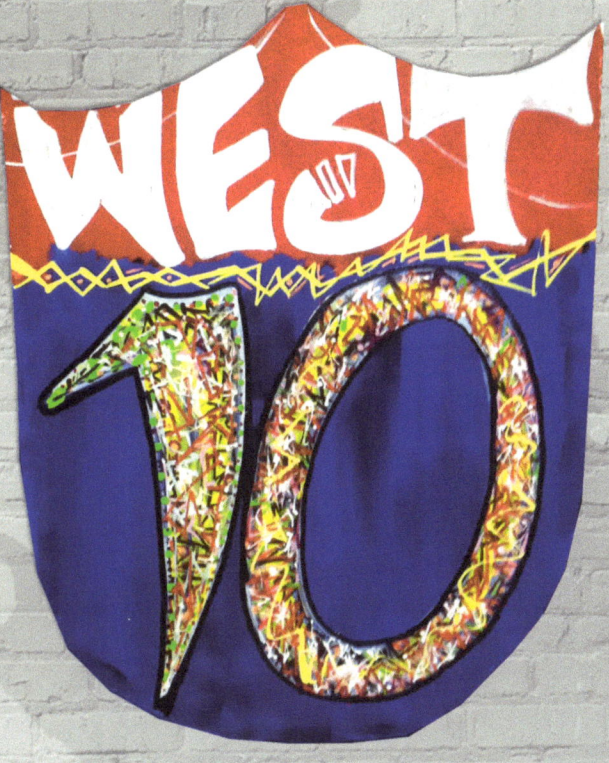

10 WEST

a collection of art & poetry

Copyright © 2015
All rights reserved.

No part of this book may be reproduced in any form or by any electronic or mechanical means including information storage and retrieval systems, without permission in writing from the author. The only exception is by a reviewer, who may quote short excerpts in a review.

Printed in the United States of America

Peace 2

D, Ms. Italy & Nino
Goldie, Rocco, Angie, Chi-town Sam
& all the artists at
Downtown Playground in Los Angeles
peace to all the wanderers
peace to all Idol smashers

CONTENTS

ADDICTS OF THE METROPOLIS

Big Face Alchemist ... 8
Deranged Love (for brooklyn) ... 9
Suicide Poem ... 10
Daft Fragments of Love ... 10
Hotbed Of Sweat (naked city) ... 11
Broken Heart Blues (Happy Valentine's Day) ... 12
Forbidden Days On Doublecross Beach ... 13
Scary Traphouse (space city) ... 14
Taco Land Eulogy ... 15
Zone 9 ... 16
Planet-X Pleasure Cruise ... 17
Vegas Blues ... 18
Car Wrecks In Our Heads ... 19
America Is Where You Create Geniuses ... 20
Blackjack Curse ... 22
Avenue Voodoo (saint elmo) ... 23

LA MENTALITY

An Angels Anthem ... 26
Angels of Skidrow ... 27
Celebrity Energy ... 28
Love The Way You Slow Dance (for stormy) ... 29
Crazy Zone (for amanda k) ... 30
Midnight Talent Search ... 30
Natalie Wood Dedication ... 31
666 (satan's locker) ... 32
New High Street Queen (for Wu Zetian) ... 33
405 Transmissions ... 34
Silverlake Sutra ... 35
Windfall Prophet (for Hank Chinaski) ... 36

Sparkle Plenty (for Lana D) ... 37
Westcoast Workflow ... 38
Santa Monica Transformers ... 39
Visions Of Venice (angel's birthday) ... 41
Temple City Samurai ... 42
Visions Of Skidrow ... 43

SOUTHCENTRAL MINDBENDER

Architecture Of Madness ... 46
American Worship Symbols ... 47
Western Exorcism ... 48
Roaring Kong The King ... 49
Psychotic Children Of Our Time ... 50
Born On Holidays ... 51
Your Weird Relationship With Money ... 52
Church Of The New Truth ... 53
Pray For The Rise Of Technology ... 54
Dead Letter ... 55
Starfuckers (for j.p. & morgan & stanley) ... 56
Headgames (X Years Later) ... 57
Star69 (secret keys) ... 58
Institutional Memory ... 59
Secular Matters ... 60
Metaphysical Matters ... 60
Isis Psychologists ... 61
Chemical Future ... 62
Scientific Definition Of God ... 63
Santas Wearing A Ski Mask ... 64
A Poem For Buddha ... 65
Amazons Drones ... 66
Sublime Cisco Streets ... 67

ADDICTS OF THE METROPOLIS

The Big Face Alchemist
(for Ben Franklin)

they cross your bridge
from all over AmericA
demolished crowds
jacked up on kilowatts
searching for spider blue
they know the downsides
of living with cameras
-skypatrol running
their plates
these are the
-CMD capitals
we watch them
fade like election ink
back in philly you would
cut the currency with the speed
of light- you're the big-face alchemist
forging delaware armor with
front street lightening strikes
turning bells into 100s
farmers 2 rebels
how many times
the chapel master
blast the fed up?
 (today) the last fragments
of industry are scalped
& modified into an
architecture of 5's
and 9's-
(today) we feel
freedom fleeting
in missing jets -
& all that new-age dope stress
creates an atmosphere of
falling crosses
building colonies of
post modern decay

Deranged Love
(for brooklyn)

rhythm devils lay down
beautiful dark spanish
blues -heart grenades
love me with telepathy
the infinite night music
cant stop the love flux
building a merry-go round
of zigzagging stars
we are rooftop skinny
dippers
under platinum jets
we worship velocity
machines
then you start begging
(blindfolded) in crazy
places
we get medieval
(all) twisted scissors
victory whips -the
black amex -
hot kisses & nasty talk
the last hammer in the
honey pot -your body
is non-stop volcano
an ocean of slick lava
TempTempTempTempT

Suicide Poem

moonchild goodbye
I guess
im floating
lower to die
on a white lake
of endless love
this is graveyard space

Daft Fragments of Love

winter lights
dim your cold
heavy hands
play wild white
blues for ghost
lonely hearts
hammer flowers
to a cross
cults rave on
karma the cure

Hotbed of Sweat
(naked city)

gag orders
small arms fire
inter-
web digital red
& blue boo-yah
all over town
dipsy & doodling
money drips
morphine pools
cellular trips
stars whipping
in the wind
liberty
whipped out
the whippy dip
soft + pink
birthday cake
whip up
delicious
hot tits feminism.

Broken Heart Blues
(Happy Valentine's Day)

they don't call it falling
 in love 4 nothing
  i've had my heart break
into the grand canyon of
my stomach &
black butterflies fly out
of my mouth
my heart shattered into
so many pieces
i threw up glass shards
that cut
worse than jealously
or an undercover text
msg.- "who was
that?" static-my
networks in knots
swarms of mood swings
confusion over
night of the comet
the night in
teriyaki madness
the nights in your
deep lotteries
empty telephones
will turn2 tombstone

here on ground zero
ghosts will come up
& grab you
i know you see the way out of here-
shopping 4 LouieV
fast food shutdown diet
comedy (extra)
rechannel by blocking
big wrist game ego tripping
school-work skipping
lovesick abortion clinic
vandalizing spree
-even if you have to go thru hell
to get there
remember the
lightening strikes of the
lovestruck
this supernatural
power we possess

Forbidden Days
On Doublecross Beach

insomniacs cant sleep
cuz they
live doublelives
no puppies &
no ice cream
fear heavy industry
beware of zero-day
as females vanish
summers disappear
our capitol is cracking
from loopholes
every idol is broken
now the metropolis
stands closer than
Columbus & his crew
1492

Scary Traphouse (space city)

we created so many barriers-
passwords
caller ID
even a chain on the door
the feedback loop became
so intense- our laptops
of doom staring down
the greasy desoto
entranceways-
radio traffic fires up
chinese speaking
in angel language
& black range rovers
circle the house
like piranhas
a pattern
develops- jackpots of joy
are crystallizing under
hobby&bush into
bad wallpaper
(a) bedroom crucifixion
& paisley bandanas-
decoy bitches cross
borders in spanish voices
end up lost -lone star crazy

Taco Land Eulogy
(for ramiro, gypsy & punkrock)

most nights
people would feed off each other
this was their cathedral and the stage
was an altar...a strange communion
mixed with bad light, joules, volts,
& afterparties-

requiem for pearl, an oak & all the outsiders

Remember bedlam and blood from the dead milkmen,
rainbow flares crossing the ripe plum sky?
Remember the crowds so wild,
the way sunshine ricochet smiles?
Let us not forget mystery dates, raging woodies,
love bubbles and freudian slips-
outcast clientele and volume swell. Remember
taking shots, nakedness and seeing things blurry-
slicked back hair and dark shades...last words
fuck you devils...skip the doors with beehive bells-
trust in love is what the fortune tells. A southside
psychic gave this to me from her book of spells,
say 3 times, "Consumed by fire the light is my child."
Paradise is a haunting familiar place. None of us saints.
Today we pray for rain, because for us,
the closest to hell we'll ever get is a south Texas hot spell.
Sirens reverb, firecrackers delay.

Quiet on championship night, suddenly
166 decibels then it was heaven amplified

Zone 9

let me tell you how 2
prepare in this life
for the journey in2 death
let me show you how
fresh blood makes
a difference
2day is the
day of deadlines
we pray with
our shirts off
4 safe passage
thru the chaos &
in this time of crisis
we ask for blessings
on our weapons
aztecs & police
angel of the poor
you raised churches
& schools by your grace
bury my bones
like contraband
fasting isn't a waste
there are no miracles
without faith
4 protection we pray 2 the
narco saints
our devotion guarantees
smuggled keys
the doorway to 1000 safe houses
......tempTempTemptWEST

Planet-X Pleasure Cruise

I see evidence
of crosses -can
smell the vandalism
 at crash sites
the rotting flesh
squishing between
our toes -the shipwrecked
become needle freaks
for the modern age

Vegas Blues

another late night
plastered on ecstasy &
free jack- my eyes are
insomnia circles- my
money is my bitch &
it feels like my head
is detached from
my body -my speech
is a spooky type anxiety
"only the atm pays"
"only jesus saves"
(the) playground laughter
fades all vega$ fake
she had a C section
so no VBAC
if your looking 4 optimism
check your astrocast
before you jump off
the stratosphere
into all that
nasdaq junk

Car Wrecks In Our Head

from enterprise
2 paradise-all you
kangaroos in
new balance know
the best surface
2 bounce is hot
asphalt- the shattered
glass looks like
perfectly scattered stars
(the) spectacular gasoline
rainbows -dust devils
& bugsplat- sidewalks
peppered with pennies
we outrun daylight
& diamonds
the fast lane-
on the southstrip
the thunder sounds
like dynamite-
 windmill- wigwam
cactus -you gotta
block that shit out
- a storm of leaves &
shredded love letters-
expelled speedball syringes
the scenic route
feel that confetti

America Is Where You Create Geniuses

muslims measure devotion
by the length of their beards
so pharaoh put flesh
on pagan kings & used
death row to smuggle moses
into science-
chinese measure progress
in the kitchen-
cooking handmade shenzhen
pandas from scratch & the
endless supply
of children growing in the
wild like revolutions-
 god measures democracy
 by the amount of (waste) or
presidents found hanging in
surgically clean condos &
modern churches measure
faith cutting up god dollars
(this makes purity weep)
we the people lay down on
corporations sacred ground
and pray-
(never let missiles break us apart)
it is written in the stars that
4 icy cosmonauts are
buried in jerusalems
     juggernaut-
end up as american gladiators

Blackjack Curse

Every 90 minutes I can see the smoke swell
From the warships in front of Treasure Island
Ordered to conserve the mutant allele in
White tigers that roam underground parking
Beneath the fashion mall where aliens pass
Out girls phone numbers in the short distance
Between this version of Paris
24-hour recess
Mathematics can't explain this
Budget suite speed demons entertain us
Cast your spell blackjack witch,
"10,000 paychecks dedicated, make me rich
10,000 lights, screaming bitch
Rapacity arrives in stealth
From this shoe six decks dealt
Cash advance, illusions of wealth
Potluck moolah melt
Depression blooms
Howard Hughes haunts these rooms
Green felt tomb
Sin is your soul mate
Ace high straight
Saving up for silicone
Elvis please pick up the white courtesy phone
Listen to the twisted bunny moan
In a symphony of money
Don't think I forgot
This is where Tupac was shot."

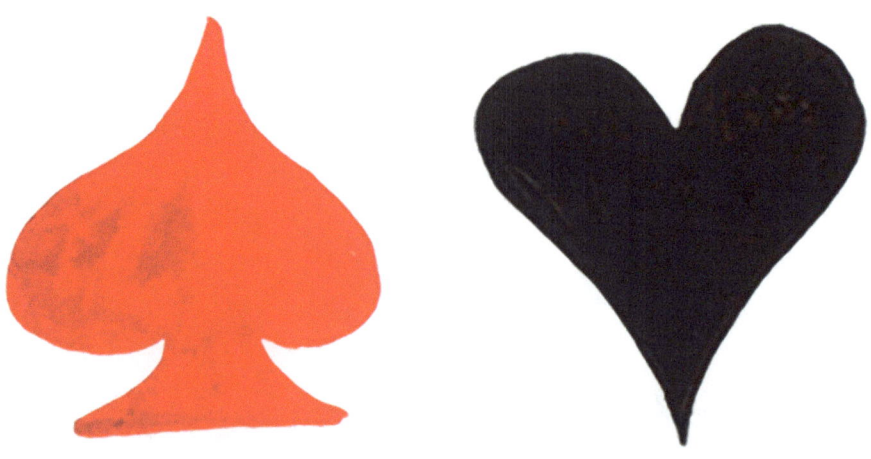

Avenue Voodoo
(saint elmo)

i see knives carving out
hysterical fantasies
& i see
blood floating needles
the slow drug
staring down into
your little bag of
skin that looks
like vacuum lint
i see black masked
fire idols everywhere
intifada screaming from
fresh newspaper clips
   the (master of the hurt)
transport dead
dolls down
 virgin river narrows
tight slick
skull fucked-
filled with freebase &
sketching over the jazz

LA MENTALITY

An Angels Anthem

I used to totally know why I did everything
that I did- but that became a dead end
no days off or nothing
no plan or benefits either
...goodbye mathematics
(now) I pledge my
allegiance to the melted
down city steel
2 chainsaws & molitovs
we ride crimewaves-cali love
the LakeShow & 10west
2 king cartel collecting dollars
in fashion district laundry
2 heat-rock who sells
rolex on elysian blocks
and my bookie
(saigon joe) at the
late night noodle spot
2 coliseum chariots
touchdowns in the circus
4 notorious & the outlaw immortals
I (carve LA on my face)
now everything blue in
westmont is bleeding vermillion-
2 avalon -disney & the whisky
(wild card gym) an opera for the poor
this is the year two thousand
& 15 (police-media-corruption)
put the whole downtown
scene under attack- union station
is our testament of tracks
2 orpheum & aerospace
the blacklist fanatics (we rowed)
spies across the river (now we float)
from southbay 2 frogtown
smashing dodger blue impalas
off echo park mansions

Angels of Skidrow
(for flower & hope)

Ur gonna text me from that distance?...
U must be up to no-good,
silly flirtations
w/smack
besides I like
being fucked up
u learn 2 flow
diamond mouth
psycho
only new snow
& long sleeves cover tracks
always pray for kids that
that fall thru cracks
we spend time scheming
new pyramids for jack
X's 2 axe
U play mercy for cannonball
on the sax - we shoot
stars
heroin (you put the hero in)
bones
dead horses (hustle quarters)
birds (we also flip them)
eight balls 4 injection
suitcases full of big medicine
put boomwaves in your
bedroom eyes lets
take the experience
beyond fantasy -it takes
(benjamins & adreneline)
when u mix
chemicals
it's them in-betweens
you sed was
permanent
vertigo........demRollin'Ryderz-Out4Action

Celebrity Energy

if iwasnt a rock star
id probably be a
serial killer...i dont want
to be alone (so)...I always
keep one in the chamber
for satan- millions of
hollow-point adderall flashbacks
advancing into long hours
of electrocution (next you)
were talking to the angels

Love The Way You Slow Dance (for stormy)

do you remember
the hustle
travelin' up & down
the 5
you told me you
were stormy
the ringleader
of lap dancers
the -(bitch killer) &
AmericA is a church
that saves us
from shivering waves
the endless night noise
cant stop cold wild spindrifts
-feelings of crystal rampage
acid meets X-ray
you sed keep going
avenida revolucion girls
-not gonna get us
show me cabo stars im crazy
in the wrong lane
tied together with
invisible ataraxy
your psycho smile
my tech9 back in your head
cobrastyle -hardcore TJ
nights- at the edge
of tenacious streets

Crazy Zone
(for amanda k)

do you remember what
pushed you over the edge?
fast curves- climax waves-
searching for breaking
points in the eyes-
the sun rushing home
the evidence of us
making love
on everything-
...I remember the knife

Midnight Talent Search
(for river)

powers of God
work hard on halloween-
from st james we sing
door 2 door (hollywood castles)
dialing up a symphony
of lit souls
this is sunsets rhythm
where the viper rises
witchfire crosses

Natalie Wood Dedication

white russian
from the valley
your nectar eyes
give angels life-
if we could read minds
it was you hiding in the
observatory the night
you circled 2 shooting stars
your wearing nothing but a smile
ready for wanderlust
in a splitsecond
forever sailaway
invincible spirit
swim calm tonight

666 (satan's locker)

I meet runaway twins on
the train to union station
they tempt me both ways
w/ blue masacra & k-k
(we play double truth) or dare
I put on black eyeliner- &
it's off w/ their underwear
I swear- shout at
the devil…they hurry me to
their storage locker or coffin…
"Do not speak evil of our king!"
our angel of execution
sings "u really have
no clue
how many
black helicopters are taking off"
when the locker opens -wet
cats claw out & butterflies turn
to dead leaves- I see
king of clubs -3 cobras
friday the 13th phobias-
we love 2 stare
at fire-
phizer, dow, love&
other drugs
this is when the physical
clocks out & we walk
around LA delusional
our ecstasy scattered like
starburst skittles orbit

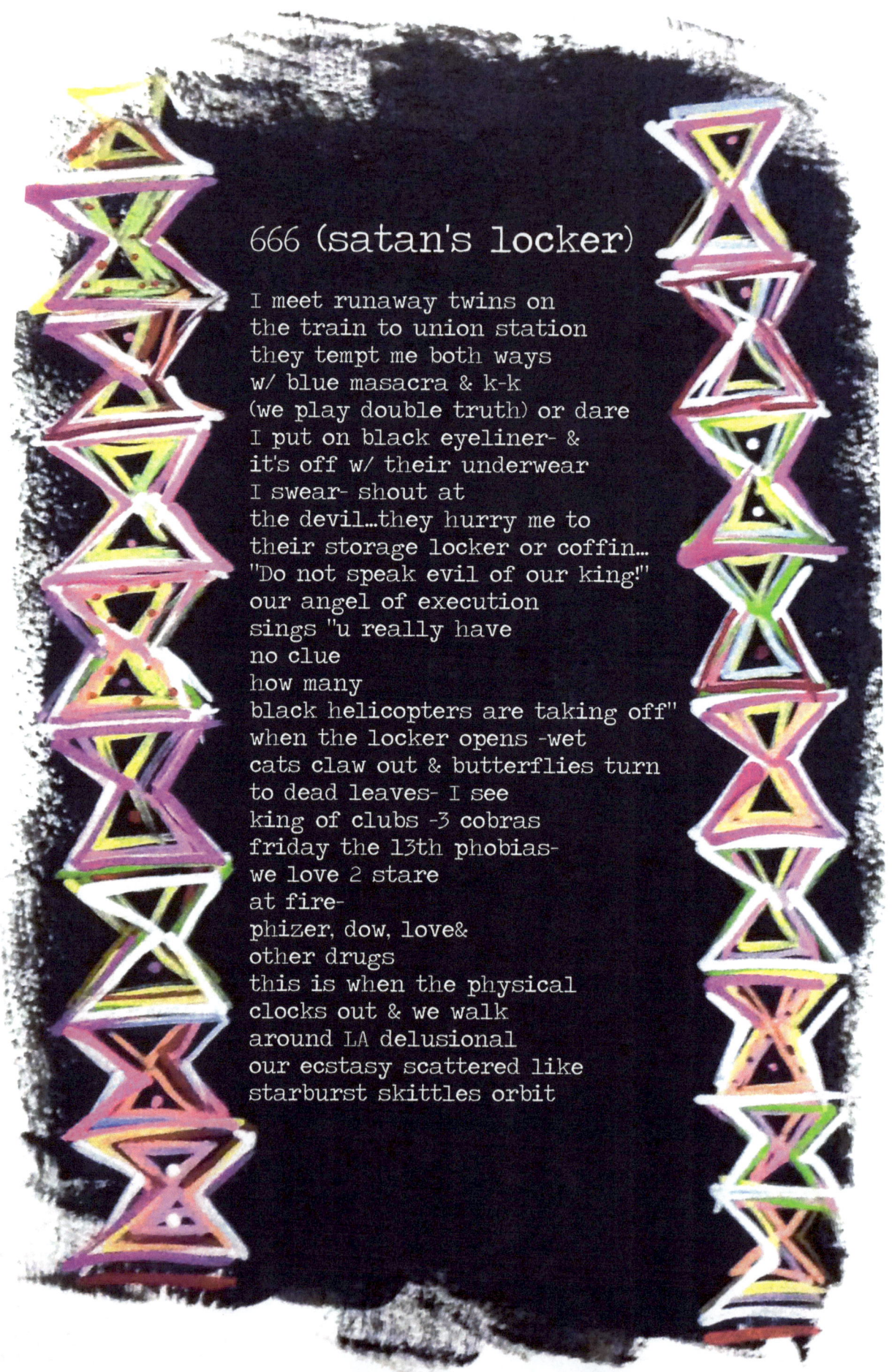

New High Street Queen (for Wu Zetian)

you made
witches breakdown
begging
for mercy
you used pretty words
for your own child
to choke upon
you went from palace
temptress to
buddhist nun
then used politics
2 flex magic on
the throne
your lovers
heads hit the floor
spit -fist
her scars scream
into fire
the demons disappear
ashes of the gladiator
transform one king
into gucci zen

405 Transmissions

the usual demons
weigh down
traffic- the 405
wakes up nasty
warped- my eyeballs
brace for jackknifed
dragons ...out here
ambulances sound like
gibbons ...and
the choir playing this
morning is the jack-hammer
this kind of gridlock
gives me jet lag
this static could use
some backward logic
the way over-pass
jumpers flatten
my emotions
I wake up in the
morning to car alarms
cuckoo w/ death rock-
kcal car chases
& crime scenes
splattered w/
hydraulics- I'm
switching lanes til
the world ends
listen 2 the bouncing soul
killer 22s - picture me rolling
on these super unleaded
streets- gold flakes mixed
in the candy paint &
rolled dice for eyes
fixed like a snake

Silverlake Sutra

brown girl
my honey
my caffeine
your bling reflects
a 1000 year old city
your smile curves
you dance nasty
2 underground
been known
to get down at
flammable liquid
raves you said
were americas
new mysticism
once in the sun
we kiss off our
clothes- add up love
(plus) all that birthday
romping -everyday
lots of cake in those
red engine jeans.

Windfall Prophet
(for Hank Chinaski)

the clock reads 8:15
3 days til xmas
woodmans luck
just rode into
the winners circle
for the last race ever
at Hollywood Park
all my beers are gone
my girl too like an errant
infield flamingo
we are fading faster
than southwest jets
so I went for a walk up Vine
to the 3 Clubs
kicking up rusty nails
& unpaid bills
see them greedy girls
make shabby love
in seedy corners
tonight peace smells
like smoke & blood
lysol & birth control
I take a seat next to
a brunette that looks a lot like my
psycho ex- (same upside down heart)
tight jeans-really smart too- both our
phones are dead so
we start talking about reality -
cotton fever & how for 70k- a beemer
is 0 street cred. we start making bets
how long it takes for a fly to land in her apple martini
how long before her sister is locked behind XanaX bars
what matters most
first kiss or last kiss
love comes when you
wish for it
wrong way to wish...WICKED STYLE HONEY RYDER

Sparkle Plenty
(for Lana D)

the drug in me is good
graceful -raised by
the funtimes in
hollywood- I long to
feel your nightmares
roar -emerge everywhere
over my holy moonlight

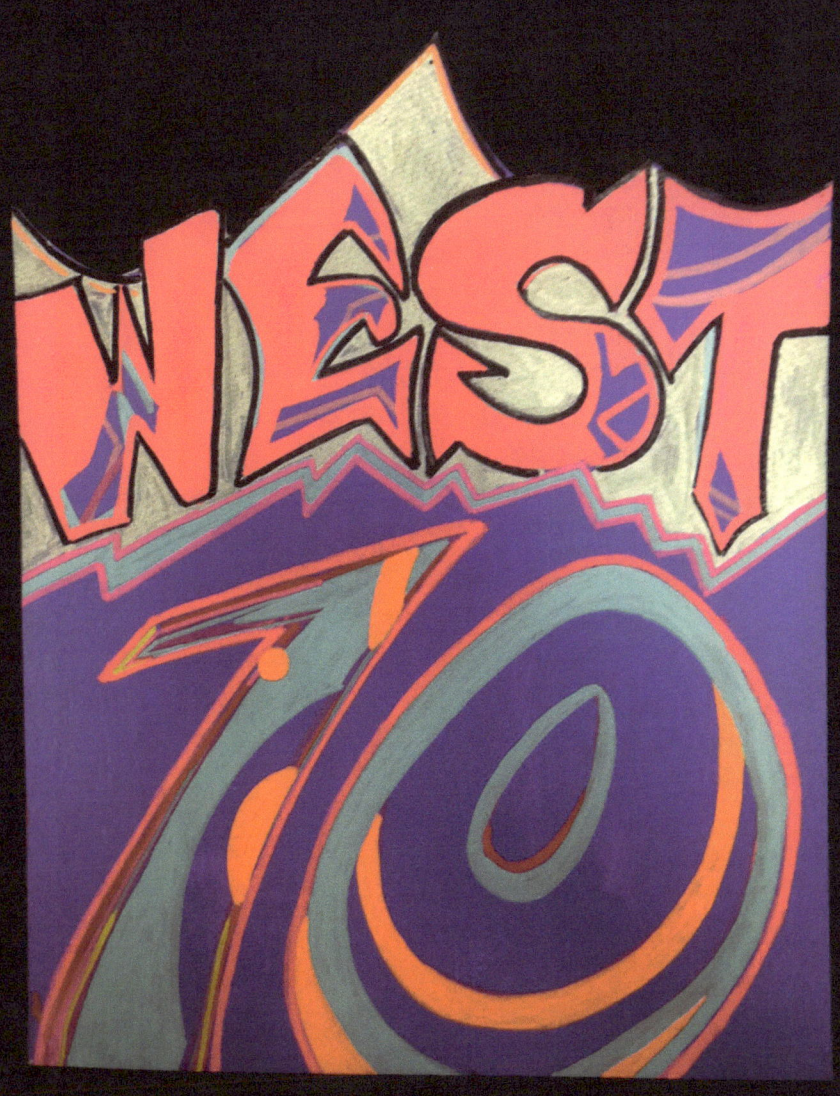

Westcoast Workflow

west coast
chevy love nothin'
but the wheel
my woman
-the sky and sand
our schoolyard
-juilliard built
her naughty body
(no more nyc drama)
now she is hermosa
illuminati & down to ride
pacific waves that shimmer
the wildlight inside her
raven eyes- the rip & tide
keep her planets bouncing
with power flowering
we go oceans deep
her body the perfect
lava & our secrets
split open -melting
the gravity between
our bodies
of raving research
...demRollinRyderz-
theCityTempts

Santa Monica Transformers

we live in a world of
fast talking women
heavy makeup
a continuous flow
of desire
(an) up all night society
flow fly flow future
love me
or don't make me
want falling in
the hungry hive
whoa...you know what
travel fast? high drags
in 7-inch heels
tonight the streets
are skintight in
day-glo bikini's
 steamy w/
lust demons
(that) illuminate
beautiful black
lips caught slippin'
under starry sheets
candy slants down
for judith priest
splash that hot
pink sequin
baked into
chiseled high
def power
tryin' ta shake
that shady enemy
with secret technique
bicycle pimps serving
up that gold glam ballyhoo
2 curbside whips-we dip low
smoking love boats...
love probably isn't
real it's like a drug- watchin'
queens gettin' loco with the cake

Visions of Venice
(angel's birthday)

your moon shapes
    create curvy fun
on what seems like today
another planet
saturated by grace
from stars-
your insane
white cake
 is our crumbling
 sacrament -
needle
thin layer of
 infinite metal
  lightning
-tracing her fragile
   come downs...tempTempTemptEmpTempT

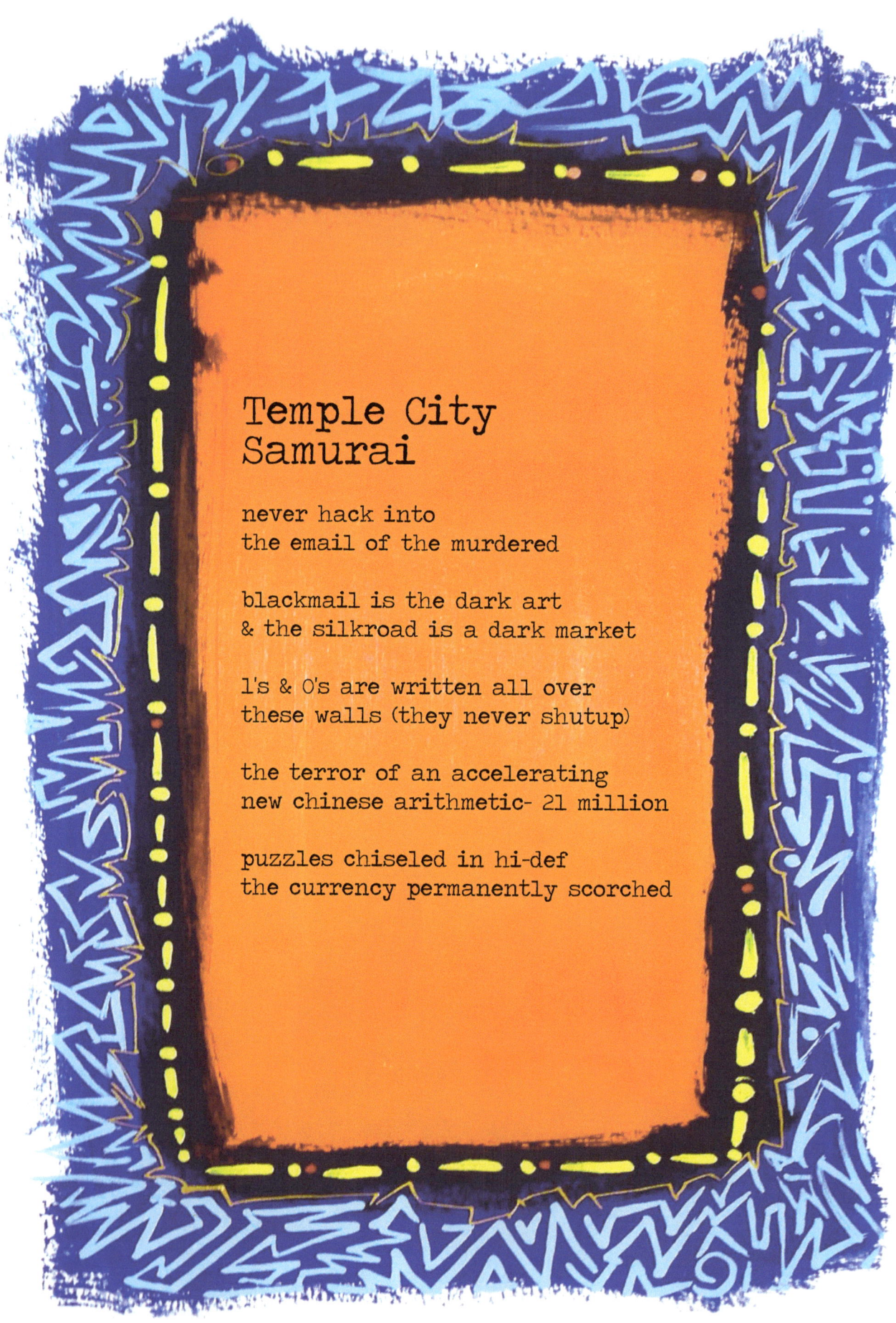

Temple City Samurai

never hack into
the email of the murdered

blackmail is the dark art
& the silkroad is a dark market

1's & 0's are written all over
these walls (they never shutup)

the terror of an accelerating
new chinese arithmetic- 21 million

puzzles chiseled in hi-def
the currency permanently scorched

Visions Of Skidrow

these days its
tough to think
more than 10 min
into the future-
out here police are
the eyes of fear
-the lizard scum-
-the breathtaking smog-
progress never comes
from the top & indian alley
 is proof (that)
    gov't is no longer relevant
-proof that they've been
planting evidence
    for a resurrection
    of inflated symbols
  & debt is the sacrifice
to this peculiar point system
 every vision an
attempt to reassemble
real truth
      shall we gather
the blasted shards
from these imacculate LA trophies

SOUTHCENTRAL MINDBENDER

Architecture Of Madness

this is 4 the unborn children
way out in time-
they are already
complaining about
the frequencies
coming from you-
so much hot excess
is yours- (the endless speed)
the screaming queen
fucking with everybody
the noise will take you 2
new levels of psych-trauma
beware of hydrogen & bombs
atoms evil messiah will
crucify their stems 2 the
flesh of new sleeper cells
splitting personalities
sky high - IQ's & angels
will rise from the broken DNA
revolutions are rolling
in the deep dancing
death of seasons
psychic agents
take back days
watch the stars
shake zion up

American Worship Symbols

first take your hearts
out of the safe
deposit box &
scratch out god
from the starcrossed
map of our soul-
apple is omnipresent
the green skin
our rebirth-
shell is hell &
adderall is our
energy policy
 -red bull is
seminole blood
on hardrock casinos
blue state is the stepped on
anthrax sent 2 democrats
our wisdom comes from
snapchats & face books
creating a world of dropouts

Western Exorcism

allah plays his games
with car bombs-
we play ours in the cold months
when a woman
will be elected president -
(a day) centered on
 her own obsessions
 -we nail your hands
    exactly where
Jesus doesn't want
 -a nirvana junkie

Roaring Kong The King

as you climb macau's
ecosystem of wealth
you will one day reach
a virtual nation- where
hong kong god's are
cloned in secret
harmony-
 a sacred vertigo
will run the planets

Psychotic Children Of Our Time

raven sez 100%
of Institutions
invent products
not the muckety-mucks
the higher ups
a continuous flow
of desire
raven sez don't
get caught in
gain & loss
you will be a slave
2 ur mind
so recognize
the illusion
& embrace it
but raven didn't make
the salary structure
he just gave it a ride
the desert is high &
wide with many
party scenes
to drop out of
raven sez economists
love finding
patterns
like predicting
lightening blackouts
or
cyclone touchdowns

Born On Holidays

-when abstract ideas
 begin to look obsessively
 at their own image-
a currency frozen on
the edges of
presidents
a midnight kiss
the evidence-
fire-up fireworks
for candles-
we pray on election day
& spend xmas in casinos
we back up beer
with irish whisky
now get naked
& parade

Your Weird Relationship With Money

try the word freedom
when you punched it in
all the information was erased
now rest your head on the moon
watch U$
throw tomahawks from 50 miles out
snow quiets the black sky
white bread makes us wonder
y you won't get social secruity
if your head still works
y vampires in the valley
flip birds
y it takes more faith
2 believe in atheism &
where will they bury the lehman bodies

Church Of The New Truth

in the west we believe
in the fine tuned armor of
democracies machines
who controls the technology
of labor?... visa is a symbol
like fixed zero -mendax surfs
darknet chatrooms with
hawala passwords 2 hack
into the vaticans secret vortex-
technology is the artifact
broadcasting the moon's
long memory 2 ivory shrines
in black washington
or opt out
and bomb islam
sail up unlimited nation
there is so much
sex in zen

Pray For The Rise Of Technology

Today let us pray for all the plankton
buried in oil fields
Today let us pray for the battlefields
sprinkled with fallen stars
Today let us pray for the cracked capitols
insane idols- for fukushima winter
malicious logic in clouds
-the climate of falling prices
Today we pray for the superstitions
-surrounding money-splitting new atoms
Today let us pray for DNA on a blade
china- pyramids- & wizards of oz.
the false prophet silenced by
calculus- show us the glory
in folding a flag
Today let us pray for a resource based
economy- the wind and waves
buddha flows like derivatives
Today let us solve the question of
fusion reaction so the petroleum kings
become extinct
tying off that dinosaur
Live from iraq

Dead Letter

Prosecutor sed
do u have a breaking point?
"I shot my fear in the face."
Prosecutor sed where do u operate?
"A fucking star."
Prosecutor sed what are yr motives?
"Im on a series of tangents my whole life."
Magistrate sed like a path to nowhere?
"In a dream the sands and dunes fall
intentionally 2 the desert floor."
Magistrate sed nothing-nowhere-no blood
Nothing written on the walls? "Systems may crash
because of their addiction 2 energy."
Female Prosecutor sed why do people
tend to sexualize everything?
"One should express pure violence with tenderness."
Prosecutor sed this question that led 2 disaster
"Is Israel real?"
Female Prosecutor sed what is the weapon of choice?
"Tax rackets, scary pumpkins and the dmv."
Hot Brunette Juror sed what did the fortune cookie say?
"Caffeine makes me yawn all the seals&salmon
died thanks to eXXon."
Prosecutor sed was it quantum suicide or suicide circle?
"I find faith in sunrise. I find moon in mythology."
Prosecutor sed do you live in the zone all the time?
"Wild expansion, then crash." Prosecutor sed r we on
the eve of universal change? "We have no beliefs only instincts."
Prosecutor sed do u know famous emily rugburn?
"Almost jane austen." Prosecutor sed what is
annihilated antimatter? "X taste like hairspray."
Prosecutor sed why does mlk blvd run thru
every ghetto of americana? "Because life moves
fast on the perimeter." Magistrate sed how did you
get thru the fake checkpoints?
"It tells a lot to read the walls of a city."
Female Prosecutor sed illusions or traditions?
"Yesterday's gone zeitgeist."
Female Prosecutor sed when's the spaceship
gonna appear? "Its here in the shape of a pentagon."
Prosecutor sed what r today's laws? "Extinct."

Starfuckers
(for j.p & morgan & stanley)

Raven stares over
the traffic wondering
how(the) big houses have
the best hackers
why management is
always changing
& from up here
the bees look like
dead astronauts
an entire galaxy
collapsed

Headgames
(X Years Later)

She seduced all of us
we knew...
we didn't give a fuck
cuz artists read the language
of the outer
relate it to the inner
weird presence of
hacker weirdoz
diet coke
coke diet
coke is the ultimate
capitalist
flatten everything
send tax money upstairs
tylenol became life savers
pretty soon we started
buying her version
our skin
the holy body
is mind-boggling
she makes it
4 US
we bought from her
collective nervous breakdowns
with her came
rare desert rain
a return to k-os
realizing the antichrist

Star69
(secret keys)

money-calculations-sun
mercury-circles-fire
moons-move-oceans
god-bondage-chaos
meditating overtime
on the steps of
science & sabbath
for strength-
pray in the wrong direction

Institutional
Memory

john was a baptist &
a scientist
born in
a small town
called dollar
where sun worship
is your idea of
something holy

Secular Matters

we talk smart-
nasa data
deepwater horizons
-bulldozing trees
 -today we breathe
a modified atmosphere
& today Detroit is in
BK orbit-

Metaphysical Matters

the truth travels from
backstreet Beirut
to front page news-
(the) mq-9 reaper
no witnesses
asymmetrical
blood splattered
syringa's
splash....out4action

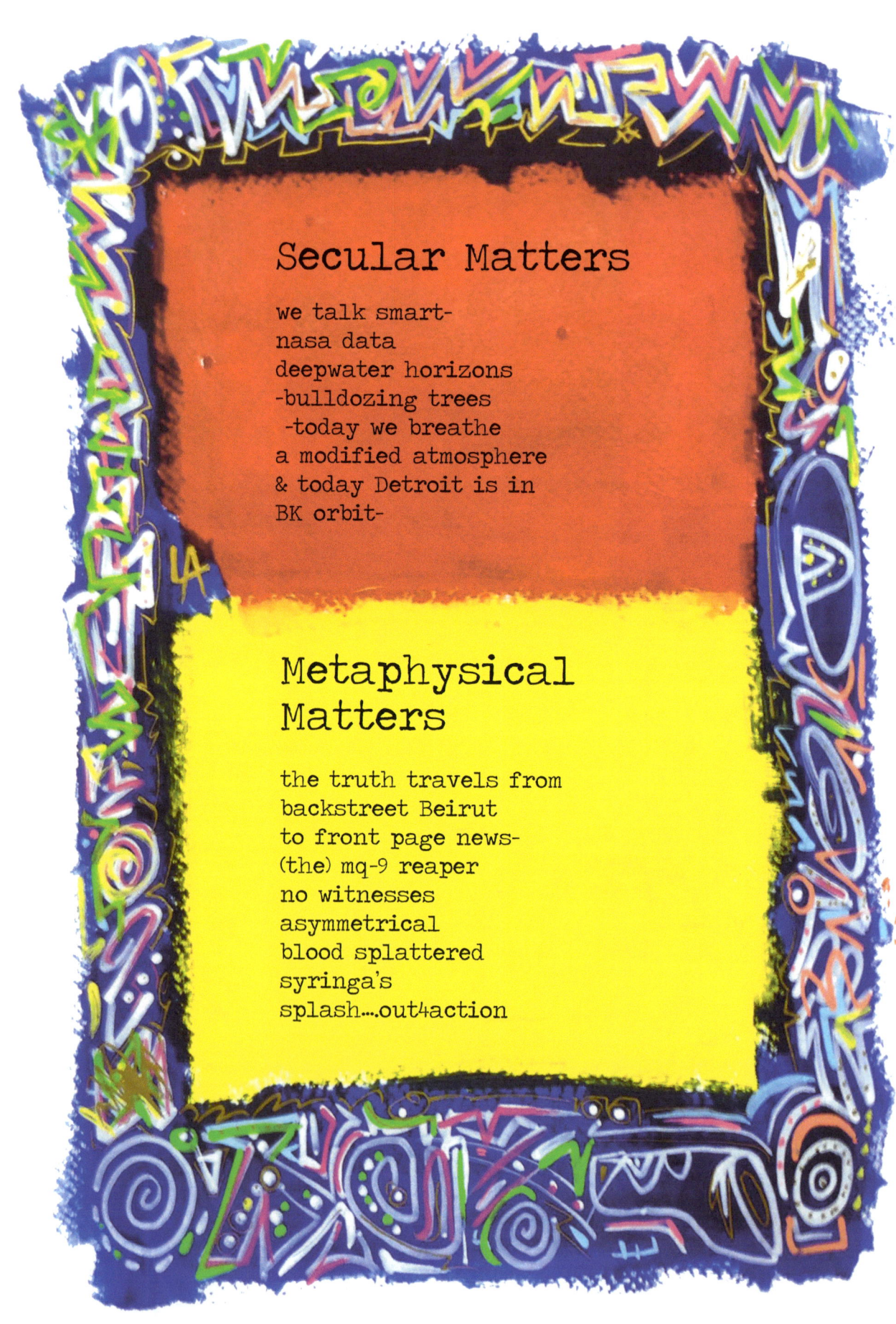

Isis Psychologists

you have no background
you have no creed
you wont pray with us-
you wave a black flag
in your courtrooms
speak to me...
(you) who keeps secrets
is it allah
putting war equipment
in your mouth?

Chemical Future

I see
narcotic god
in test tubes
I see embryos
in the black galaxies
of the soul
I see
post human
google brain

Scientific
Definition
of God

things we push 2
the recesses of our
minds resurface
like going into
the woods & gettin'
naked
felt good

Santas Wearing A Ski Mask

its noisy said owl speaking
from the future skyrocketing
utopia
           125 million holidays have
passed   climb limbs
candy tree
speech graffiti   vandalism professor
warning   a woman said science is
a university sanitizer
          dayshift 2 graveyard
$uzi lit the sky up with dynamite
cameras in the snowflakes catch
an eerie night-time collision
 of 2 sleighs &
$uzi satisfying her own self

Amazons Drones

she would encode
intelligence within
her music
then pass it off as
a secret dance
to honeybees
seducing us with
that androgynous
police voice-
scanning hard drives
for the queens asylum

Sublime
Cisco Streets

honey dove
my heart is dropping
in dolores park acid
lets tumble in the temple
wicked naked (press play)
& thrashing back at her
secret pad- (golden gates)
therapy for us
is screwed
every chance
we kiss kiss
love her wonder &
overjoyed in her
new rivers

Joe Wright is a full spectrum writer
expanding the dimensions
of Los Angeles' new language.

10westla.com

www.ingramcontent.com/pod-product-compliance
Lightning Source LLC
Chambersburg PA
CBHW042002150426
43194CB00002B/98